SEARCH AND SEE

Bible Heroes

Stephanie Jeffs
Illustrated by Roger Fereday

Scripture Union

CONTENTS

ADAM
The beginning of everything GENESIS CHAPTERS 1:1 – 2:3 4

NOAH
The great flood GENESIS CHAPTERS 6:9 – 9:17 6

ABRAHAM
The stars and the promise GENESIS CHAPTERS 12:1-9; 15:1-6; 18:1-15 8

JACOB
A terrible trick GENESIS CHAPTERS 25:19-34; 27:1-45 10

JOSEPH
The jealous brothers GENESIS CHAPTER 37:1-36 12

MOSES
The hidden baby EXODUS CHAPTER 2:1-10 14

JOSHUA
The walls that fell down JOSHUA CHAPTERS 2:1-22; 5:13-15; 6:1-23 16

SAMSON
The strongman JUDGES CHAPTERS 13:1-5; 16:4-30 18

DAVID
The giant-killer 1 SAMUEL CHAPTER 17:1-50 20

ELIJAH
Fire from heaven 1 KINGS CHAPTER 18:16-39 22

DANIEL
The den of lions DANIEL CHAPTER 6:1-28 24

JONAH
The man who ran away JONAH CHAPTERS 1–4 26

ANSWERS 28

SEARCH AND SEE

Bible Heroes

What evil creature is hidden in a tree in the Garden of Eden?

What is a shadoof? Or a shekel?

How many wild animals can you see hiding in the hills?

Who killed a giant with a small stone?

Who was so strong he pulled down a Philistine temple?

Who got swallowed by a big fish?

The answers to all these questions, and many more, are hidden in the twelve action-packed pictures and stories about Bible heroes in this book.

Read the story... Look at the pictures... Hunt for the clues... On every page there's plenty to Search and See!

P.S. If you get stuck, the answers are at the back.

ADAM
The beginning of everything

GENESIS CHAPTERS 1:1 – 2:3

At the beginning of the world there was nothing and there was nobody. There was only God.

Suddenly God spoke. 'Let there be light!' he said. Immediately light shone. God took the light and made it into day, and he took the dark and made it into night.

God spoke again. Each time he spoke, he created something new. He made the sky, and wrapped it round the earth. He made the rivers and seas, and separated them between the land. He filled the earth with plants and trees, and gave them seeds, flowers and fruit.

God made time begin. He made the sun, the moon and the stars, and he placed them in the sky.

God brought life to the earth. He made every living creature, from the birds which flew through the air, to the fish in the sea, and the animals that scampered and slithered on the land.

God was pleased with everything he had made. And then he made his finest creation – the first man and the first woman, called Adam and Eve. They were like God – able to think and feel and love. He gave them a beautiful garden in which to live, and called it the Garden of Eden. God made Adam and Eve to be his friends, and to care for everything that he had made. God knew that his creation was very good.

He put Adam and Eve in charge. He told them to tend and care for the animals, and to work the land. They enjoyed being with God, in the beautiful garden.

'You can eat from any of the trees in the garden,' said God, 'apart from the tree of the knowledge of good and evil. If you eat from that tree, our friendship will be spoiled and you will die.'

There was so much in the garden to choose from: different plants and flowers, different seeds and fruit. Everything was theirs. They could have whatever they wanted. But Adam and Eve chose to disobey God, and when they did, their friendship with God was spoiled.

1 God made the sun and the moon. Can you find them?

4 God made the tiniest insect as well as the largest animal. What is the biggest creature you can see? And the smallest insect?

2 Adam and Eve were asked by God to look after the garden and everything in it. What work are they doing?

3 The rivers and the seas were full of fish and living creatures. Find a frog.

5 God made all the plants. Can you find some oranges, apples and grapes?

6 The tree of the knowledge of good and evil was in the middle of the garden. What creature is hidden in that tree?

NOAH
The great flood

GENESIS CHAPTERS 6:9 – 9:17

As the years passed, more and more people lived on the earth. They did what they wanted, they did bad things and they forgot about God. It made God very sad.

There was only one man in the whole world who was good. His name was Noah and he was God's friend.

'I am sorry that I made the world,' God said. 'I will destroy it. But I will save Noah and his family.'

God told Noah his plan. 'I want you to build a boat,' he said. 'I will give you the exact details. I am going to flood the earth with water, but I promise that you and your family will be safe.'

Noah built the boat out of cypress wood. He built three decks, divided them into rooms, and covered the outside with pitch to make it watertight.

'Find two of every living creature,' said God to Noah. 'Take them on board the boat with you and your family. Then I will flood the earth.'

Noah did as God asked. It began to rain. It rained for forty days. The rivers burst their banks, and the seas gushed across the land. Soon the whole earth was covered with water. Everything was destroyed. But Noah and his family were safe.

Many days later the rain stopped. The waters began to go down. The boat rested on land.

Noah took a raven, and set it free. But the raven flew backwards and forwards over the water because it had not found anywhere to rest. Noah sent out a dove, but it quickly returned.

Noah waited. After seven days he sent out the dove again. This time it returned with an olive leaf in its beak. Noah knew that the waters were disappearing. A week later, when the dove did not return, Noah knew that it was safe to leave the boat.

'Come out of the boat,' God told Noah, 'and enjoy the earth.'

Noah, his family and the animals left the boat. Immediately Noah thanked God for keeping them safe.

'I promise never to flood the earth again,' said God. 'I will put a rainbow in the sky so that you can remember my promise.'

1 Noah had three sons called Ham, Shem and Japheth. Find them and their wives in the picture.

4 Some animals have camouflage to help them hide unnoticed. Can you find a tiger? And two chameleons?

2 God made all the animals. Find the biggest and the smallest animal in the picture.

3 Noah took two of every animal into the boat. Sometimes male and female animals look different from each other. Can you see a male and female lion, a peacock and a peahen and male and female birds of paradise?

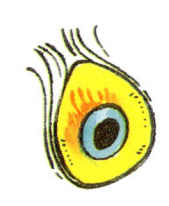

5 Find the dove with the olive leaf and the raven.

6 The rainbow was a sign that God would never flood the earth again. Can you name the colours?

ABRAHAM
The stars and the promise

GENESIS CHAPTERS 12:1-9; 15:1-6; 18:1-15

There was once a man called Abraham who came from the big city of Ur. As a young man he went with his father and brother to a place called Haran.

Years later, God said to him, 'I want you to leave Haran and go and live in a new place. I will make your descendants into a great nation. I will show you where to go.'

Abraham obeyed God. He told his wife, Sarah, what God had said. Abraham packed all his possessions and, together with his servants and all his flocks of sheep and goats, began to travel towards the west.

When at last he arrived at the land of Canaan, God spoke to Abraham again. 'This is the land I will give you,' he promised. 'And I will make you and your descendants into a great nation.'

Abraham was surprised. He and Sarah had no children, and now they were old.

'How is this possible?' Abraham asked God. 'Sarah and I are too old to have children now.'

'I promise that you will have a son of your own,' said God. He took Abraham outside. It was night, and the sky was full of stars. 'Look at the stars and see if you can count them,' said God. 'You will have as many descendants as there are stars in the sky.'

Many years passed and Abraham settled in Canaan. He became a wealthy man. He had many sheep and goats and lots of servants. But still he did not have a son.

One day he was sitting outside his tent when he noticed three strangers standing nearby. He stood up to greet them, and offered them food and water which was the custom.

The men sat down in the shade. 'By this time next year you will have a son,' they said.

Abraham knew that his visitors had been sent by God and that God would keep his promise. Sarah was not so sure. She laughed when she heard what they said. She thought that she was far too old to have a baby.

But God kept his promise. One year later, Abraham and Sarah had a son. They called him Isaac.

1 There were no shops. Find someone weaving cloth to make clothes, grinding corn to make bread, and milking a goat.

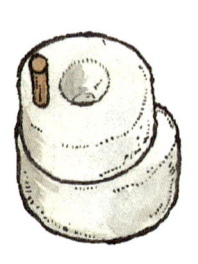

3 Find the well in this picture. What was used for carrying water?

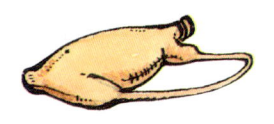

2 Abraham and Sarah and their servants lived in tents. Which one is Sarah's tent?

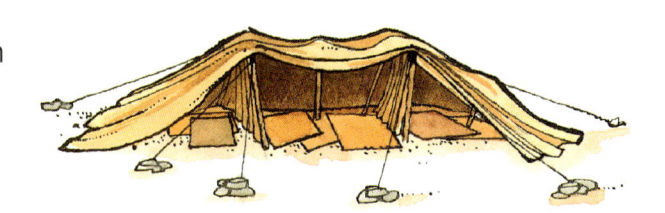

4 The place where Abraham lived was called Mamre. It was famous for its great trees. How many different kinds of trees are there?

5 Abraham was rich. He did not have lots of money. He had lots of sheep and goats. What else in the picture tells you he was rich?

JACOB
A terrible trick

GENESIS CHAPTERS 25:19-34; 27:1-45

Abraham's son Isaac married Rebekah. They had twin sons, Esau and Jacob. Esau, the eldest, was strong and brave, an outdoor man with hairy arms. He was a skilled archer and a good hunter. He was Isaac's favourite. Jacob was quiet and preferred to remain at home: he was Rebekah's favourite. She wished that Jacob could receive all the rights of the first-born son, instead of Esau.

One day Esau returned home from hunting. He was hungry. Jacob, who had stayed at home, was cooking some stew.

'Give me something to eat,' said Esau. 'I'm starving!'

Jacob took his time. 'Only if you give me your first-born son's rights to our father's property and money,' he said.

'Agreed,' said Esau. All he wanted was the stew.

Years later, when Isaac was very old and almost blind, he knew he was about to die. He wanted to give Esau the special blessing for the first-born son before he died.

'Go and hunt some wild game, and cook it for me,' Isaac said to Esau. 'Then I will give you my special blessing.'

Esau took his bow and arrow and left the tent. He did not know that Rebekah had been listening.

'Now is your chance!' she told Jacob. 'Kill one of the goats, and I will make your father's favourite meal. Pretend to be Esau, and your father will bless you instead of him.'

Jacob was uncertain. 'Esau is hairy,' he said. 'Even though Father cannot see clearly, he will know when he touches me that I am not Esau.'

Rebekah was prepared. She gave Jacob some of Esau's clothes, and tied goatskin on his hands and neck.

'Father, it's me, Esau,' lied Jacob, as he took the meal in to his father. Isaac heard Jacob's voice, but when he felt the goatskin, he was sure it was Esau. He ate and drank, and then he blessed Jacob.

Jacob left and Esau arrived. 'Here I am, Father,' he said.

Isaac trembled when he realised what he had done. He could not give Esau the special blessing as well.

'Jacob has tricked me!' cried Esau angrily. 'I will kill him!'

Rebekah warned Jacob and he ran away from home.

1 Find Esau in the distance. What sort of wild animal is he hunting? What weapons did he use?

4 The Bible says that Jacob cooked Esau some lentil stew. Find the lentils drying in the sun.

2 People slept on a padded mat on the floor of the tent. What did they do with it in the daytime?

3 Flocks of sheep and goats provided milk, cheese and meat. Animal skins were used to make tents and wool was woven for clothes. Find someone milking a sheep, and someone weaving wool.

5 Isaac and his family were living at a place called Beersheba where his father, Abraham, had dug a well. Can you see the well in the picture?

6 How many things can you see which would be used for cooking and for making bread?

11

JOSEPH
The jealous brothers

GENESIS CHAPTER 37:1-36

1 The pit the brothers put Joseph in was used to store water, but was empty. Can you find it?

Jacob was a rich and powerful man. He owned many flocks of sheep. He had two wives, twelve sons and a daughter. But one son he loved more than all his other children. This was his second youngest son – Joseph.

Joseph knew that he was his father's favourite. Jacob did not hide it from his other sons – he gave Joseph a special multi-coloured coat. Joseph had strange dreams which made him appear important, and he boasted to his older brothers about them. They hated Joseph.

One day, Joseph's older brothers were looking after their father's sheep far away from home. Jacob sent Joseph to see them. When they saw him walking towards them they said, 'Let's kill him! We'll tell our father that he was attacked by a wild animal.'

Reuben, the eldest brother, hesitated. 'Don't kill him,' he said, 'just throw him into this pit.' He hoped to rescue him later.

As soon as Joseph arrived, the brothers grabbed him. They ripped off his multi-coloured coat and threw him into the pit. Then they sat down to eat, before deciding what to do next.

Suddenly they saw a group of traders in the distance. Their camels were laden with spices, balm and myrrh. They were going to Egypt.

'Why don't we sell Joseph, rather than kill him?' Judah asked. The brothers agreed, and as soon as the traders came along, they pulled Joseph out of the pit, and handed him over for twenty pieces of silver.

They smeared animal blood over Joseph's special coat. Then they went home and showed it to Jacob.

'Joseph has been torn to pieces by a wild animal,' cried Jacob, and nobody could comfort him. For years Jacob grieved over Joseph's death. He did not know that his son was alive. But years later there was a terrible famine in Canaan and so Jacob sent his sons to Egypt to buy food. It was there that they met Joseph again. God had looked after him and brought him success. He had became Pharaoh's second-in-command and Governor of Egypt.

4 Which wild animals can you find in the picture?

2 What were the camels carrying on their backs?

3 A shepherd had to protect his sheep from attack. What weapons did he use?

5 Find Joseph's special coat.

6 Joseph was sold for twenty silver pieces called shekels. Can you see them?

MOSES
The hidden baby

EXODUS CHAPTER 2:1-10

Many years after the time of Joseph and Jacob, there were lots of God's people, the Israelites, living in Egypt. At first, the Egyptians had welcomed the Israelites, but now they were worried – there were just too many of them. So the Pharaoh made the Israelites work as slaves, making bricks out of mud. Then he issued an order saying that all Israelite baby boys should be killed at birth.

There was an Israelite woman called Jochebed who had a baby boy. She kept him hidden for three months at home but he was getting too big – and too noisy – to hide. So she made a basket out of reeds, made sure it was watertight, and put her baby in it. The baby's sister, Miriam, took the basket and hid it in the reeds by the side of the River Nile.

An Egyptian princess was walking by the river with her attendants. She heard the sound of crying and saw the basket. When she saw the baby she felt sorry for him, and wanted to look after him.

Miriam watched carefully. She came out of her hiding place. 'I know someone who could look after him for you until he is older,' she said to the princess, and ran to fetch her mother.

'Let me give you some money for doing this for me,' said the princess to Jochebed. 'I will call the baby Moses.'

So Moses grew up with his mother until he was old enough to be looked after by the princess. God watched over him. He had chosen Moses to be a great leader. When Moses grew up he would lead the Israelites out of slavery in Egypt to the Promised Land of Canaan.

1 The basket was made out of strips of reeds. How many other things can you see made out of reeds in the picture?

4 The Israelite slaves were forced to make bricks. Can you see how these were made?

2 The Egyptians used a shadoof to take water out of the River Nile. It was a long pole with a bucket on one end and a weight at the other. Can you see one in the picture?

3 Miriam is hidden in the picture. Can you find her?

5 The basket was hidden in the tall reeds along the banks of the River Nile. Can you find three other things hidden in the reeds?

6 The Egyptians thought that the scarab beetle was very special. They thought that the beetles would prevent them from being ill. This is what a scarab beetle looks like. How many can you see in the picture?

JOSHUA
The walls that fell down

Joshua chapters 2:1-22; 5:13-15; 6:1-23

When Moses the great leader of the Israelites died, God said to Joshua, 'Get my people ready and lead them into the Promised Land. Be brave! I will be with you.'

Joshua came to the River Jordan. On the other side was Canaan, the land God had promised to his people. There were people already living in the land so Joshua sent two spies to gather information about the city of Jericho.

When the spies arrived in Jericho, they met a woman called Rahab. She helped them.

'I know that God will let you capture Jericho,' she said. 'Everyone knows that God is with the Israelites!'

The spies promised to keep Rahab and her family safe when they made their attack. Then they escaped from Rahab's house, and made their way back to the camp.

Joshua led the Israelites across the river. Then he gathered his army, and made his way towards Jericho.

Suddenly he saw a man standing in front of him. The man held a sword in his hand.

'Are you for us or against us?' asked Joshua.

'I am the commander of God's army,' he said.

Joshua knew then that God would fight with them.

The citizens of Jericho stayed within the city walls. The gates were tightly shut. Everyone was afraid.

'Every day for the next six days, march your soldiers once around the city walls,' God said to Joshua. 'Make seven priests march in front of the ark of the covenant, blowing trumpets, but do not speak. On the seventh day, march seven times around the city walls. Ask the priests to blow their trumpets. When my people hear the long trumpet blast, tell them to shout. Then the city walls will fall down!'

For six days the Israelites marched around the city walls. On the seventh day, they marched seven times. The ark of the covenant went ahead of them, and the priests blew their trumpets. When he heard the long trumpet blast, Joshua gave the people the signal.

They shouted as loudly as they could. Immediately the city walls collapsed and crumbled, and the Israelites charged forwards, taking the city. Only Rahab and her family were saved.

1 Rahab lived in the city walls. She told the spies that she would tie a scarlet cord in her window, so that they would know where she lived. Can you see it?

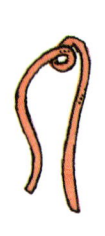

4 The trumpets were made from rams' horns. How many were there?

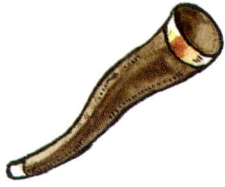

2 Rahab hid the spies under bundles of flax drying on her roof. How many bundles can you see?

3 Find the ark of the covenant. Do you know what was inside it?

5 Jericho is one of the oldest cities in the world. It was an oasis and sometimes called the 'city of palms'. Count the palm trees inside the city walls.

6 Joshua was a good leader. He was a man who listened to God and obeyed him. Can you find him in the picture?

SAMSON
The strongman

JUDGES CHAPTERS 13:1-5; 16:4-30

When an angel announced to Samson's parents that they were going to have a son, he told them to bring up the baby to obey God, and to make sure that he never had his hair cut. This would be a sign that God had chosen him to rescue his people from their enemies, the Philistines.

When Samson grew up he was so strong he could kill a lion with his bare hands and break down strong city gates with his shoulders. He frightened the Philistines.

But one day Samson fell in love with a Philistine woman called Delilah. The Philistines were delighted! They gave Delilah money to find out the secret of Samson's strength.

'Why are you so strong?' she asked him. 'What will take away your strength?'

'Tie me with seven tough bowstrings, and I will lose my strength,' said Samson. She tied him up but he simply snapped the bowstrings and got free.

Delilah asked Samson again. This time he told her that he would lose his strength if she tied him with new rope. But the new rope snapped like cotton thread. Delilah asked Samson again. He told her to weave his hair into the material she was making on her loom. But Samson broke the loom.

Delilah nagged until Samson told her the truth.

'If my hair is cut, I will lose my strength!' he said.

So when Samson was asleep, the Philistines cut off his hair. When Samson woke up, he had lost all his strength.

The Philistines seized and tortured him. They blinded him. They put him in prison. While he was in prison, Samson's hair began to grow.

One day they displayed Samson in their temple, and made fun of him.

'Our god let us capture you!' they jeered.

They put Samson between the temple pillars. Carefully, Samson stretched out his arms until he could feel them. Then he prayed, 'O Lord God, please give me my strength back.'

Samson pushed the huge pillars. Suddenly, they cracked and toppled over. The temple and everyone in it was destroyed. The Philistines were defeated.

1 A braid is like a plait. Samson had seven braids of hair. How many can you see?

4 The Philistine temple was in the city of Gaza. Lots of people travelled through Gaza on their way to or from Egypt. How many Egyptians can you see in the picture?

2 The Philistines were experts at making weapons. How many daggers and shields can you find?

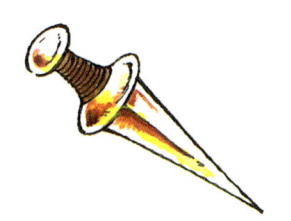

3 The Philistines worshipped the god Dagon. It is generally thought that Dagon looked half man and half fish. Can you find an image like this in the picture?

5 Samson's chains were made out of bronze. Can you find something else made out of bronze?

6 Philistine pottery was highly decorated like the pots from Greece and Crete. Find this jug.

DAVID
The giant-killer

1 SAMUEL CHAPTER 17:1-50

The Philistine army gathered across the valley and faced the Israelite army. This time the battle was different. The Philistines had a champion fighter. His name was Goliath. He was huge.

Twice a day Goliath stood and shouted across to the Israelite army, 'Send someone to fight me!'

The Israelites were terrified. No one would take up Goliath's challenge.

But one day a shepherd boy called David was visiting the Israelite camp, bringing food for his brothers, who were serving in the army. When David heard Goliath's challenge and saw how frightened the Israelites were, he was furious.

'How dare he scare the army of the living God!' said David angrily.

His comments reached King Saul, who sent for him.

'I will fight Goliath,' David said to Saul.

'But you are just a boy,' replied the king.

'I know,' said David, 'but when I look after my father's sheep, I often have to fight wild animals. God has kept me safe. He will keep me safe from Goliath.'

Saul was impressed. He offered David his own armour, but it was far too big. Instead, David took his shepherd's staff and his sling. He chose five small pebbles from the stream, and went to face Goliath.

Goliath laughed when he saw David. But David cried out, 'You may come to fight me with weapons, but I come to fight you with the living God on my side! He is the God of the armies of Israel.'

Goliath lunged forward. Quickly David took a stone and put it in the sling. The stone shot through the air, and landed in the middle of Goliath's forehead.

The huge man fell face down on the ground. David ran and stood over Goliath. The Philistine enemy had been defeated. The armies of the living God had won!

1 King Saul offered David his armour. Find it in the picture.

4 Can you see Goliath's shield-bearer?

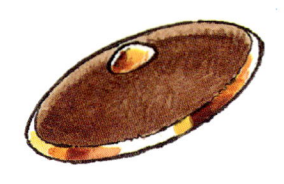

2 David had killed wild animals such as lions and bears while looking after his father's sheep. Find one of these animals in the picture.

3 Look at Goliath's helmet, armour and leg greaves (on his shins). They were all made of bronze. Can you guess how much his coat of armour weighed?

5 At this time, most weapons were made out of bronze, but the Philistines had discovered how to make iron, which was stronger than bronze. Find an iron weapon in the picture.

6 David chose five smooth stones from the stream to use in his sling. Can you find five other smooth stones, hidden near the stream?

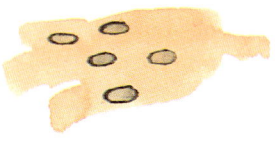

ELIJAH
Fire from heaven

1 KINGS CHAPTER 18:16-39

'You troublemaker!' said King Ahab, when he saw the prophet Elijah. 'It's all your fault that we haven't had any rain in Israel, and that our crops are dying.'

'No it isn't!' said Elijah. 'It's your fault. You are the king of Israel, yet you and your wife Jezebel have disobeyed the true God and have worshipped Baal instead. Meet me on Mount Carmel. Summon all the people to come, and bring Jezebel's prophets with you!'

Ahab sent the order throughout Israel. Everyone gathered on Mount Carmel. Elijah stood by himself.

'We'll have a contest! The prophets of Baal can prepare a sacrifice for their god, and I will prepare one for mine. Instead of setting light to our sacrifices, we will ask our gods to send down fire. The one who sends down fire must be the living God.'

Two bulls were chosen for the sacrifice. First, the prophets of Baal gathered round Baal's altar. They called and they shouted to their god, 'O Baal, send down fire!'

Nothing happened.

'Perhaps Baal's asleep?' suggested Elijah. 'Or maybe he's popped out for a while. Why don't you shout a little louder?'

The prophets of Baal grew desperate. They shouted and danced, but still nothing happened.

By the end of the day, Elijah spoke to the people. 'Help me mend God's altar,' he said.

Elijah arranged the wood and the sacrifice on top of the altar. Then he dug a deep trench around it. 'Pour water over the altar,' he said. Three times the people drenched the altar.

Then Elijah prayed. 'I am your servant. I have done everything that you have asked. Now please show everyone that you are the living God.'

Immediately, the altar burst into flames. Everything was burnt – the wood, the sacrifice, the stones and the ground.

The people fell on their knees. 'Elijah's God is the living God!' they cried.

After that, rain fell on the land once more. Three years of drought had ended.

1 There had been no rain in Israel for a number of years. How many signs of the drought can you see?

4 Elijah told the people to fill four large jars full of water. Three times the people drenched the altar. Find the jars in the picture.

2 Elijah travelled throughout Israel on foot. Can you see two things he needed on his travels?

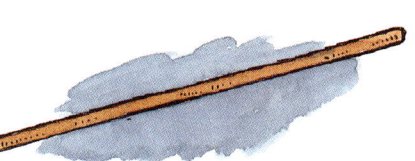

3 Can you find King Ahab's chariot?

5 Can you find King Ahab in the picture? Look at his face. How do you think he is feeling?

6 Some people in the crowd have brought idols with them. Can you find them?

23

DANIEL
The den of lions

Daniel chapter 6:1-28

There was once a man called Daniel, an Israelite living in Babylon. He was a captive of the Babylonians and had been chosen to serve King Darius of Babylon. But even though Daniel lived and worked in a foreign country, he never forgot the living God.

King Darius saw how clever Daniel was, and how hard he worked. He knew that he could trust him so Darius decided to put Daniel in charge of his whole kingdom.

The other officials were amazed. They were jealous of Daniel, and tried to think of a way to disgrace him. At last they said, 'We will never find anything wrong with Daniel, unless it is something to do with the way he obeys his God.'

Suddenly they had an idea. They went to King Darius and said, 'Issue a decree that no one must worship anyone but you for the next thirty days. If they do, they will be thrown into a den of lions.'

King Darius was flattered by this suggestion and agreed that the decree be published.

When Daniel heard what the king had said, he went up to his room, and opened the windows that faced towards Jerusalem. Then he knelt and prayed to the living God. He prayed three times a day, just as he had always done.

Daniel's enemies were delighted. They told the king of Daniel's disobedience.

King Darius was very unhappy. He knew that Daniel was a good man. But the law could not be changed.

'May your God save you!' said the king, as he ordered Daniel to be thrown into the lions' den.

He sealed the den, and returned to his palace. He was so upset, he could not sleep.

In the morning King Darius rushed to the den. He called out, 'Daniel, has your God saved you?'

'Yes!' shouted Daniel. 'An angel came and shut the lions' mouths. They could not hurt me!'

Darius was delighted. 'I will issue another decree,' he said. 'From now on, everyone in my kingdom must worship the living God!'

1 Look at the lions' den. There is a gallery around the top. How many people can you see standing there?

4 Daniel had some friends who had also come from Israel. Like Daniel, they prayed to the living God. Can you see them?

2 There is a door in the side of the den. How many seals are there on the heavy stone door in the picture?

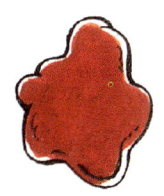

3 King Darius employed court musicians. Can you find one of them?

5 King Darius lived in a palace. Find a rooftop garden, two fountains, three servants, and a golden statue of Darius.

6 How many lions are there in the picture?

25

JONAH
The man who ran away

JONAH CHAPTERS 1–4

Jonah was a prophet, one of God's special messengers.

One day God spoke to Jonah. 'I want you to go to Nineveh, and tell the people that I have seen how bad they are. Tell them I will punish their disobedience.'

But Jonah did not want to go to Nineveh. Instead, he ran away in the opposite direction to the port of Joppa. He found a ship bound for Tarshish – as far away as possible from Nineveh. He paid his fare, and went on board.

But Jonah could not run away from God. God sent a strong wind to whip up the waves. The wind blew, and rain began to fall. The waves rose and fell. The ship was in the middle of a violent storm.

The sailors were afraid. They clung to one another, and prayed to their own gods. They threw their cargo overboard, but still the ship began to sink.

The sailors went to find Jonah. He was asleep below deck. 'How can you sleep,' asked the sailors angrily, 'when we are all going to die? Pray that your God will save us.'

The sailors were desperate. They knew that someone was responsible for causing such a sudden, violent storm. They drew straws. Jonah drew the short straw. Jonah was the one.

'What have you done?' they asked.

'I have run away from the living God,' said Jonah.

The sea grew rougher, sending the ship high into the air.

'Throw me overboard,' said Jonah. 'Then the sea will become calm.'

The men tried to row for the shore, but it was useless.

'Living God,' they cried, 'forgive us for killing this man!' They threw Jonah into the sea. Immediately the sea grew calm.

As soon as Jonah hit the water, he was swallowed by an enormous fish. While inside the fish, Jonah realised how foolish he had been.

'I am sorry,' he cried to God. 'Help me!'

Three days later, the big fish spat Jonah out of its mouth on to dry land. This time, he went to deliver God's message to Nineveh.

1 Can you find the straws the sailors used to find out who was the man causing the storm?

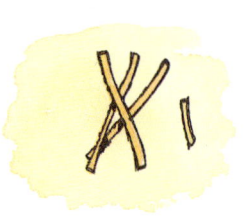

4 Jonah paid to travel on the ship. Find the sailor who has a purse full of money on his belt.

2 Look in the sea. What sort of cargo was the ship carrying?

3 The Bible does not tell us what sort of fish swallowed Jonah. There are all sorts of big fish in the picture. Which one do you think it would be?

5 When the storm was at its worst, the sailors asked their own gods to help them. Can you find two of them?

6 Most ships carried some animals to provide milk and food during the voyage. Can you find two different sorts of animal on board the ship?

27

ANSWERS

ADAM The beginning of everything
pages 4/5

1

2 They are growing plants for food.

3

4 The rhino is the biggest; the dragonfly is the smallest.

5 The oranges and grapes are in the basket. The apples are on the tree on the right.

6 There is a snake hidden in the tree of the knowledge of good and evil. The Bible tells how God's enemy, in the form of a snake, persuaded Adam and Eve to disobey God. This spoiled their special friendship with God and was the first time anything bad had happened in the world.

NOAH The great flood
pages 6/7

1 Noah and his wife are in the centre of the picture. All the other people are his sons and their wives. God promised to save Noah and his family from the flood. Through their descendants God promised to make a new beginning on the earth.

2 The elephant is behind the ostriches; the mouse is next to the peacock.

3

4 The hidden tiger is to the left of the camels. The chameleons are hiding in the grass.

5 The olive leaf that the dove brought back from the olive tree was a sign that there was new life on the earth. In many countries, the olive leaf is a symbol of peace.

6 The colours of the rainbow are: red, orange, yellow, green, blue, indigo, violet.

ABRAHAM The stars and the promise
pages 8/9

1 The wool for making clothes came from the flocks of sheep and goats. It was woven and then made into clothes. Corn was ground between two stones to make flour for bread. Goat's milk was also made into cheese.

2 The tent is in the centre of the picture.

3 Water was collected in a leather bucket. It was stored in animal skins.

4 The big trees are evergreen oaks; the tall trees are poplar; and the others are willow. Nomads like Abraham settled near water, which they needed for themselves and their animals. In this part of the world, trees were often a sign of a good water supply.

5 Abraham had many servants, and donkeys and camels as well as flocks. This shows he was rich. At this time, there was no system of buying and selling using coins or metals for money.

JACOB A terrible trick
pages 10/11

1 Esau is hunting a deer with a bow and arrow. People hunted fallow and roe deer, gazelles and ibex, as well as partridges, for food.

2 The bedding mat was rolled up in the daytime.

3 All the clothes were woven by hand, using wool from goats or sheep. Milk could also be made into cheese.

4 Lentil stew and bread would be an everyday meal. Meat was for special occasions.

5 The well is at the top of the picture. Beersheba is thought to mean 'the well of seven lambs'. It was on the trade route to Egypt and the southernmost town in the land.

6 To make bread you would need: some grain, and a mill to grind it into flour, some water and perhaps salt, and some yeast (or a bit of leftover dough from yesterday's bread was usually kept). Then you would need a fire with a hot, flat stone to cook the bread on. Bread was usually made into round, flat loaves.

JOSEPH The jealous brothers
pages 12/13

1 The pit is in the centre of the picture. Pits were used to store water in the desert in the dry season. They had a narrow entrance, but widened out underground, and were quite deep. If the pit had been full, Joseph would probably have drowned.

2 The traders were carrying spices, balm and myrrh, carried in large leather bags on the camels.

3 A shepherd used his stick (sometimes called a staff) both to fight with wild animals such as lions and bears, and to help rescue his sheep. He could throw stones very accurately with his sling.

4 There is a jackal and a wolf in the picture. At this time lions, bears, wolves and jackals lived in the wilder parts of the country, so a shepherd had to be always ready to defend his sheep against predators.

5 Although Joseph's coat is often described as 'multi-coloured', it may have been a special coat with long sleeves or decorated with embroidery.

6 A shekel was not a coin, but a block of silver. It weighed about 11gm.

MOSES The hidden baby
pages 14/15

1 The papyrus reeds which grew by the river could be made into lots of things including boats and baskets, which you can find in the picture. The most important thing the Egyptians made out of papyrus was paper.

2

3 Miriam was older than Moses. She was brave to offer to find someone to look after the baby for the princess; and clever to fetch her own mother. Later, when the Israelites slaves escaped from Egypt Miriam had to obey her little brother Moses, the leader of God's people.

4 The bricks were made out of mud or clay, water and straw. The mixture was pressed into a wooden 'form' and then left to go hard in the hot sun. Many buildings in Egypt were made of these bricks.

5 There is a fishing line, a water jar and a cat with kittens. The Egyptians who lived near the Nile depended on the river for food, including fish, and water. The Egyptians loved cats. Some of the gods they worshipped took the form of cats.

6 There are six scarab beetles in the picture.

JOSHUA The walls that fell down
pages 16/17

1 Rahab is listed in Matthew's Gospel as one of the ancestors of Jesus.

2 There are three bundles of flax. Flax is a plant with brilliant blue flowers. It is used to make linen; and the seeds make oil.

3 Inside the ark of the covenant were two pieces of stone with the Ten Commandments written on them.

4 There were seven trumpets.

5 There are five palm trees. Archaeologists have found evidence of settlements at Jericho dating back to 8000 BC.

6 Joshua became leader of the Israelites when Moses died. He had come to Canaan, the land God had promised to his people, on an earlier mission as a spy when he was a young man.

SAMSON The strongman
pages 18/19

1 Three braids are visible.

2 There are four daggers and three shields. The Philistines were the first people in this area to discover how to make iron. This meant that their weapons were better and stronger than the Israelites' weapons. The Israelites fought many battles with the Philistines to gain control of the Promised Land.

3 The Philistines, like many people, worshipped idols made out of wood, metal or stone. God told the Israelites that they were not to worship any god made like this. They must worship the Lord God, who made the world, but could not be seen.

4 There are three Egyptian travellers.

5 Food offerings were made to the idol Dagon in his temple.

6 The Philistines were sometimes known as the Sea People because they had originally come across the Mediterranean to Israel. This probably explains why remains of their pots found in Israel are similar to pots found in Greece.

DAVID The giant-killer
pages 20/21

1 When David tried on the king's armour it was so big and so heavy that he could hardly stand up. David was so confident in his own skill and in God's power, that he went to meet Goliath without any armour.

2 There is a lion on the top of the cliff. Lions were quite common in David's time. Assyrian kings kept lions in pits and would throw criminals or people they did not like into the lion-pit to be killed.

3 The Bible says that Goliath's coat of armour weighed 57kg/125lb.

4 The leader or king in the battle always had someone who went before him holding his shield. Goliath's shieldbearer is standing behind him!

5 Goliath's spear has an iron tip. Iron weapons were better and stronger than bronze weapons.

6 David knew exactly what sort of stones to choose because he had already killed a number of wild animals with his sling.

ELIJAH Fire from heaven
pages 22/23

1 The signs of drought are the dried-up ground, the trees with no leaves on and the skeleton of a dead animal.

2 Elijah took with him his staff (stick) and his cloak.

3

4 There are four large water jars.

5 King Ahab was probably very angry and also frightened. He was a weak king because he did not worship God properly and allowed his wife Jezebel to worship idols and false gods.

6 There are four idols hidden in the picture. God had told his people not to worship idols made of metal, clay or wood. They were to worship only him – the living God.

DANIEL The den of lions
pages 24/25

1 There are thirty-three spectators. Seeing people eaten by lions was a spectator sport in Babylon, but King Darius had left Daniel overnight in the den, with nobody watching.

2 There are three seals on the door. Sealing the door was a way of making sure that no one else opened it while the king was away.

3 The musician is carrying a lyre, which was a sort of harp.

4 In another part of the book of Daniel, three Israelite friends of Daniel were thrown into a furnace because they refused to worship a statue, and God saved them.

5 Babylon was a wonderful city, full of great buildings and a centre of learning. Kings often displayed golden statues of themselves.

6 There are three lions. The lions would have been very hungry. Daniel reports that God sent an angel to keep their mouths shut because God knew that Daniel had not committed any crime.

JONAH The man who ran away
pages 26/27

1 Another way of drawing lots was to have a number of numbered stones in a bag, and for each person to take one out of the bag without looking, to see who was 'it'.

2 The ship was carrying wine, crates packed with bottles of oil, sacks of grain and other goods.

3 The Bible does not actually say that Jonah was swallowed by a whale, but the sperm whale in the picture has a throat large enough to swallow a man.

4 The sailor with the purse is holding on to the mast.

5 These idols – gods made of metal or wood – were no help in the storm. Only God could do something about it.

6 There are some chickens and a goat. A goat would be used for milk, and a chicken for eggs. The chicken could also be used for meat.

31

Published in the UK by Scripture Union
207–209 Queensway, Bletchley, Milton Keynes, Bucks MK2 2EB
ISBN 1 85999 235 8

First edition 1998

Copyright © 1998 AD Publishing Services
Illustrations copyright © Roger Fereday

All rights reserved

Printed and bound in China